C

MW01224593

A Step by Step Guide on how to Master the Art of Quilting With Several Techniques and Practical Projects to Make You a Professional Quilter

Monica Steve

Table of Contents

CHAPTER ONE

INTRODUCTION

The blankets in the V&A's assortment length the household and the expertly made, reflecting various uses and relationship throughout the hundreds of years in which they were made and gathered. In the case of uncovering choice embroidery methods or a brief look into the lives of the individuals who made and utilized them, these are objects that reward a more critical look.

As a method, quilting has been utilized for a differing scope of items, from garments to many-sided articles, for example, pincushions. Alongside interwoven, quilting is regularly connected with its utilization for bedding. Be that as it may, blankets are not just functional items. The blankets in our assortment have been safeguarded for a wide range of reasons, regardless of whether wistful or dedicatory, as instances of embroidery abilities and procedures, or even on account of the particular textures utilized in their plans.

What is quilting?

Quilting is a technique for sewing layers of material together. Despite the fact that there are a few varieties, a blanket for the most part implies a bed blanket made of two layers of texture with a layer of cushioning (wadding) in the middle of, held together by lines of sewing. The lines are typically founded on an example or plan.

The historical backdrop of quilting can be followed back at any rate to medieval occasions. The V&A has early models in its assortment from Europe, India and the Far East. The word 'quilt' – connected to the Latin word 'culcita', which means a support or pad – appears to have first been utilized in England in the thirteenth century.

The soonest quilting was utilized to make bed blankets: fine blankets are regularly referenced in medieval inventories and much of the time turned out to be family legacies. Since their commencement, numerous unrivaled instances of the strategy have made due by being gone down through ages. Presently in our assortment, the Tristan Quilt gets by from thirteenth century Sicily. It portrays 14 scenes from the medieval legend of Tristan and Isolde – exuberant delineations of fights, ships and strongholds – and is one of the soonest enduring instances of 'trapunto', or stuffed quilting, (from the Italian 'trapuntare', to knit).

During the medieval period, quilting was likewise used to deliver attire that was light just as warm. Cushioned wear could be put on under protection to make it progressively agreeable, or even as a top layer for the individuals who couldn't bear the cost of metal shield.

One fine case of stitched garments in our assortment is an Indian chasing coat, made in the seventeenth century, when the Mughal tradition governed South Asia. The perfect 'tambour' binded line (worked from the top surface with an exceptional needle called an 'ari', like a sew snare) recommends that it was presumably crafted by a master create workshop that would deliver work for fare toward the West just as for the Mughal court.

Quilting lines

In spite of the fact that quilting can simply utilize fundamental running fasten or backstitch, each line must be made exclusively to guarantee it gets all the layers inside the blanket. Where the sewing is set down in improving examples, it very well may be incredibly fine work. Famous sewing designs have been given names, for example, 'Broken

Plaid', 'Hanging Diamond', 'Turned Rope' or 'Genuine Lovers' Knot'.

Since things, for example, bed blankets ordinarily include enormous surface regions, quilt making is frequently connected with social events where numerous individuals share the sewing. Especially in north America, where early pilgrims from England and Holland built up quilting as a mainstream create, there is a convention of a blanket creation 'honey bee' for a young lady going to get hitched, with the point of sewing an entire blanket in one day. One American 'Lady of the hour's Quilt' in the assortment was made for the marriage of John Haldeman and Anna Reigart in 1846. It utilizes an example known as 'sunburst' or 'rising sun', mainstream for its representative relationship with the unfolding of another day.

Quilting in Britain

In Britain, quilting was generally famous in the seventeenth century, when it was utilized for sewed silk doublets and breeches worn by the affluent and later for slips, coats and petticoats. Blankets were created expertly in significant towns and urban areas London, Canterbury and Exeter are completely connected with rich models in our assortment.

Blankets were likewise imported. Knitted Indian bed blankets produced using chintz texture (Indian painted and colored cotton) were extremely well known fare things for both the British and Dutch markets in the late seventeenth and eighteenth hundreds of years.

Quilting likewise has a local history. Huge numbers of the English stitched things in the Museum's assortment are crafted by ladies sewing locally for their own utilization. While some were made by need, others were made to check explicit life events, for example, a birth or wedding, or, similar to the

Chapman quilt, were maybe made for a settlement.

What is interwoven?

Albeit firmly connected to quilting, interwoven is an alternate embroidery procedure, with its own unmistakable history. Interwoven or 'punctured work' includes sewing together bits of texture to shape a level structure. In Britain, the most suffering technique is known as 'piecing over paper'. In this strategy, the example is first drawn onto paper and afterward precisely cut. Little bits of texture are collapsed around every one of the paper shapes and attached into place (otherwise called seasoning, this uses long, brief join that will in the long run be expelled). The shapes are then combined from the back utilizing little join called whipstitches.

In the event that quilting is regularly connected with warmth and insurance, interwoven is all the more firmly connected with household economy – a method of spending pieces of textures or of expanding the working existence of apparel. In contrast to quilting, interwoven stayed a transcendently residential, as opposed to proficient, undertaking. Not all interwoven was created for reasons of economy, notwithstanding.

There's proof that a portion of the interwoven blankets in our assortment utilized critical measures of extraordinarily purchased textures and these blankets have been ascribed to white collar class ladies making these articles for delight as opposed to need. There was additionally a convention of military blankets, sewn by male troopers while posted abroad in the second 50% of the nineteenth century.

The Museum at first gathered instances of interwoven in light of the essentialness of the sections of materials, as opposed to the functions overall. Therefore, our assortment diagrams the utilization of the fine silks and velvets of the seventeenth and eighteenth hundreds of years through to the modest cottons made during the Industrial Revolution. The biggest number of interwoven blankets in our assortment date from the nineteenth century. During this period, many-sided plans were utilized to depict various themes – from sacred text and scriptural scenes, as observed in Ann West's blanket, to scenes of world occasions and in any event, playing-card structures, as found in a bed blanket dated to 1875 – 85. This sort of interwoven was famous to the point that few models were shown at the Great Exhibition of 1851.

During a similar period, interwoven was advanced by any semblance of jail reformer Elizabeth Fry as an aptitude that ought to be educated to female detainees – a methods for giving the detainees both work and permitting time for reflection. This custom has as of late been revived by social undertaking Fine Cell Work in a coordinated effort with the V&A and the detainees of the HMP Wandsworth Quilt.

Interwoven saw a wide decrease over the twentieth century, yet was received by the style business during the 1960s as a 'look' related with flower child culture, not only a method. Before the century's over, both interwoven and quilting – as specialties so firmly connected with ladies – became procedures utilized by craftsmen, for example, Tracey Emin and Michelle Walker to investigate thoughts of 'ladies' specialty' and work. Memoriam by Michele Walker is one model in our assortment. You can likewise watch interviews with contemporary craftsmen and blanket creators Jo Budd and Natasha Kerr who draw on the long convention of quilting and interwoven for their contemporary craftsmanship practice.

CHAPTER TWO

TYPES AND EQUIPMENT

Various sorts of quilting exist today. The two most comprehensively used are hand-quilting and machine quilting.

Hand quilting is the route toward using a needle and thread to sew a demonstrating join to hand over the entire domain to be sewn. This ties the layers together. A quilting packaging or band is oftentimes used to help with holding the piece being sewn off the quilter's lap. A quilter can make each participate thus by first driving the needle through the surface from the right side, by then pushing it back up through the material from a wrong side to complete the line; this is known as a cut join. Another decision is known as a shaking secure, where the quilter has one hand, regularly with a finger wearing a thimble, on the cover, while the other hand is arranged underneath the piece to push the needle back up. A third option is assigned "stacking the needle" and incorporates doing in any event four lines before getting the needle through the texture. Hand quilting is up 'til now practiced by the Amish and Mennonites inside the United States and Canada, and is getting a charge out of a resurgence around the globe.

Quilting machine in Haikou, Hainan, China

Machine quilting is the route toward using a home sewing machine or a longarm machine to sew the layers together. With the home sewing machine, the layers are joined together before quilting. This incorporates laying the top, batting, and pulling out of a level surface and either staying (using colossal self locking pins) or joining the layers together. Longarm quilting remembers putting the layers to be sewed for a phenomenal edge. The packaging has bars on which the layers are moved, keeping these together without the necessity for connecting or staying. These edges are used with a specialist sewing machine mounted on a phase. The stage rides along tracks so the machine can be moved over the layers on the edge. A longarm machine is moved over the surface. On the other hand, the surface is gone through a home sewing machine

Tying is another procedure of appending the three layers together. This is done on a very basic level on quilts that are made to be used and are required quickly. The strategy of tying the sweeping is done with yarns or various strands of string. Square packs are used to finish the ties so the cover may be washed and used unafraid of the bundles coming undone.[36] This system is by and large called "connecting." In the Midwest, joined bed covers are suggested as couch beds.

Quilting is as of now educated in some American schools. It is in like manner taught at senior rotates around the U.S., yet quilters of all ages go to classes. These sorts of workshops or classes are moreover open in various countries I in social orders and junior schools.

Contemporary quilters use a wide extent of quilting plans and styles, from old and ethnic to post-current present day models. There is no one single school or style that manages the sweeping creation world. In spite of capacity level, all quilters know the criticalness of having the right instruments when quilting. Having the right gadgets extends the fluid method of causing a to sew and can even be improved after some time with preparing. Having the right gadgets will increase profitability and make the quilting experience one to review. Coming up next is an overview of the different gadgets and tips that can be used to make a cover by hand or machine

Sewing machine

A respectable quality sewing machine is a helpful extension to the route toward sifting through a sweeping top. Some furthermore use a home sewing machine for quilting together the layers of the cover, similarly as confining the last thing. While for all intents and purposes all home sewing machines can be used to weave layers together, having a wide throat, the space aside of the needle part, is incredibly helpful in light of the fact that it is less difficult to control an awkward cover through the machine when the throat is both high and long. It is basic to perceive how your particular model limits in order to pick the correct settings, string the needle and bobbin, and work the machine. Here is a useful guide on using a machine.

- **Fabric Markers or Ruler**

When making a sweeping it is basic to check the surface that you are cutting in order to have a heading when cutting the surface, or you could use a quilting ruler and rotational shaper. While meaning the surface it is urged that you use a surface marker, which is a marker that washes out when the sweeping is washed or will obscure away after reiterated washes.

- **Longarm quilting Machines**

The longarm quilting machine makes it more straightforward to make greater covers considering the comprehensive arm that is used. Having the choice to utilize the greater machine and not holding the material that is being used while quilting empowers the methodology to move along significantly snappier and makes it less complex on the quilter.[38] Some sweeping shops offer longarm organizations, where one can pay for their endeavor to be sewn and every so often, bound as well.

• Machine Quilting Needles

When quilting, one of the most noteworthy instruments that is used is the needle. Whether or not you are quilting by hand or by machine, the needle that is being used is essential to the decisive result. Using an unseemly needle can incite puckering, thumps, or even the material being torn. Machine quilting needs a sharp needle to adequately cut the three-segment quilt sandwich and suitably sew together the sweeping top, batting and backing.

- **Hand Quilting Needles**

The traditional needles used for quilting are called betweens and are regularly humbler and more grounded than customary sewing needles. They have an incredibly little eye which prevents any extra thump at the pioneer of the needles when you are overcoming the thread.

- **Pins and Thimbles**

Perceiving how pins and thimbles work is furthermore critical during the time spent creation quilts. A wide scope of mixes of staying can be used all together get near results and the empowering part is understanding existing blends similarly as preparing new ones. Thimbles are not required at this point are valuable for keeping fingers safe.

• **Threads**

Picking the right sorts of strings for a cover can be irksome and students may require some assistance from a master or further created quilter. The concealing, course of action, and sort of string that is used will have a basic activity in the aftereffect of the last quilt.[38]

• **Rotary Cutters and Boards**

What a quilter uses to cut the surface is a urgent development in the quilting technique. It is huge each piece is completely balanced to prevent a disproportionate or chaotic appearance and to thwart alter. Rotational cutters changed quiltmaking when they appeared in the late 1970s. A rotating shaper offers even the shakiest of hands the ability to make incredible, even cuts and constrains the chance of goof

• **Quilting Templates/Patterns**

Covers can have a wide scope of designs or models and they can largy influence the definitive result. There are different mediums that can be used and depending upon the use, size, and style they will give your cover a moved look. Arrangements are generally seen as the reason of the structure of the sweeping, like an arrangement for a house. At whatever point used fittingly it can help quilters with making a cover of their getting a charge out of and give them a sentiment of satisfaction and vision for future sews they have to make.

CHAPTER THREE

HINTS FOR SEWING DIFFERENT QUILT SEAMS

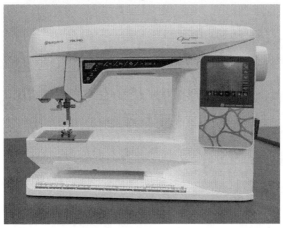

We ought to just get this out in the open. I castigated you to clean those surfaces yesterday – the cutting table, the squeezing board, and the sewing table. For the most part, those surfaces in my studio are really perfect a tolerable bit of the time.

Regardless, I have another game plan of work tables and this is the thing that they take after.

Ideally, this destruction would be repressed. In any case, it's assuredly not. I'm endeavoring to control myself on starting anything new or pulling something out of the closet. I keep figuring how lovely it would be if I didn't have to get anything off these tables with the ultimate objective for people to come and sew.

From the time that this picture was taken and today, there's been a huge change in that mess. I've filtered through endeavors, some of which I've arranged and will manage during my sewing significant distance race. In any case, really – in what manner may one work with this kind of destruction on each surface? It's inconceivable. In case you don't have plans to manage a specific endeavor – I suggest getting a few boxes and perfectly pack it away (named clearly).

The cleaner the workspace, the more positive it'll be to work. Additionally, if you have a mind boggling sewing machine like the Opal 690Q essentially remaining there? Taking everything into account, that is a goliath squander. We ought to sew continually and using our gadgets.

A normal sight in a quilter's studio – the dreaded "beforehand" picture

I thought we'd see some different sorts of wrinkles that you'd run into while piecing a sweeping top, similarly as some expansive tips for a logically beneficial day.

1. Hold the strings or strings

Exactly when you start to sew something, hold those thread(s). In case you use the Scissors Function, you shouldn't have a bobbin string to hold, anyway you'll have a top string. Hold that string as you sew. If you don't, it'll make an enormous home of string underneath your work. Looks loathsome and obfuscated.

Then again, you start sewing on a bit of surface and a short time later chain piece into your endeavor.

Since we're contributing the vitality on our endeavor and we Since we're contributing the vitality on our endeavor and we have an unbelievable sewing machine to work with, we should cause the endeavors as smooth and great as they to can be.

Hold the strings when you're starting a different line of sewing.

2. Edge control

In the event that you're adding edges to a sweeping, help yourself out and measure through the point of convergence of the cover. Use that estimation to cut the edges.

In that capacity, the two side edges should be a comparable length and the top and base edges should in like manner be a comparative length as each other. Why? If you essentially start to sew an edge strip onto your sweeping, there's an incredible chance that the two edges won't end up being a comparative length. One side of the cover may have expanded a little piece more than the other and it's a given that the sides have broadened more than the inside has. This breezes up giving the edges fairly a wavy edge, especially if there is more than one periphery on the cover.

In the photo underneath, you can see I'm using those work tables (I unveiled to you they looked altogether better from when that first picture was taken) to spread out my edge strips. I'm using my assessing tape to help with cutting both side edges to a comparative length.

Doing this helps with ensuring the cover will be straightforward with 90-degree corners. This is a fundamental development to ensuring your sweeping hangs straight and level.

Using an evaluating tape to cut edges to fit a cover

Since those periphery strips are a comparable length, they may not fit flawlessly to your cover. This is the spot staying comes in. I don't stick anything when I piece a square. Regardless, I pin my edges always.

It is definitely not a brilliant idea to run over the pins when sewing. Pin from the side with the pioneer of the pin standing apart creation the pin easy to grab and empty as you sew.

To precisely stick a periphery, arrange the point of convergence of the edge to the point of convergence of the cover and pin the concentrates together. By then arrange the pieces of the deals to the pieces of the deals. Pin and straightforwardness in the sweeping top or the periphery so they fit.

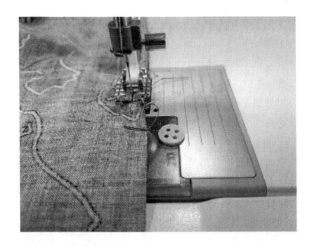

Detect your pins with the pioneer of the pin watching out to make the ejection of the pin less complex.

3. Guide your work

You must reliably be holding and controlling your work. You don't need to push and pull (aside from in case you're going over a lot of mass and a short time later at times the machine may need a smidgen of support), anyway under average sewing conditions, you ought to just oversee. I truly direct the pieces with two hands. The left hand sits near the needle and associates the surface and deals with the mass on the left, while my right hand is masterminding the two edges of the surface. I don't sew without in any occasion one hand on the work.

It's extremely ordinary for people to draw near to the completion of a wrinkle and let go of what they're sewing as they pursue the accompanying piece. You're mentioning bother when you do this as the wrinkle settlement will go wonky. Do whatever it takes not to do it! Much equivalent to you wouldn't take your hands off the managing wheel since you showed up at your garage.

You can see that I'm using the edge of the Quilter's ¼" Piecing Foot as the guide for my wrinkle settlement. It's a simple assignment to get a definite wrinkle reward.

Use two hands to coordinate the work. No convincing motivation to push and pull. Chain piece where possible

Instead of break the string, I've used one of my ender/pioneer pieces to keep the chain (of the string) going. I'll insert the accompanying undertaking piece straight up to the needle once my triangles have cleared the needle.

Having the Sensor Foot and the Needle Up/Down limit on the Opal 690Q makes chain piecing a snap. I quit sewing, the presser foot raises imperceptibly and I can set the accompanying piece straightforwardly against the needle. You can go snappy with this segment and still get wrinkles that are magnificently orchestrated close to the beginning and end of each wrinkle. A seemingly insignificant detail yet a HUGE differentiation in the idea of work.

Using an ender/pioneer close to the completion of the wrinkle to not break the string

5. Use a fair shade of string

Remember yesterday I discussed the shade of string I use? It's a light diminish. OK have the option to see any light diminish in this wrinkle? No – the strain is so impeccable on the Opal 690Q (and no modifying was basic). Consistently, I've seen understudies fight with the strains on their machines. In case you don't appreciate the strain, by then you should get acquainted with progressively about it.

Take some time one day and play with the weight – start at the most secure strain (9.8) and work your way down to zero strain.

See what happens with the underside of the line and besides what it looks like on the top. At the point when you understand this thought, you'll have the alternative to sew anything.

None of the diminish string used to line this wrinkle shows up on the exterior of the work

6. Using the line plate as the wrinkle control

Out of nowhere, I like to offer the wrinkle room on my sweeping sponsorships more broad than ¼". If the wrinkle is legitimately in the point of convergence of the sponsorship, that wrinkle can take a huge amount of abuse when the sweeping is crumpled since most covers get fallen in the inside.

Guarantee that you expel the selvages of the sponsorship pieces you will sew. It's never a savvy thought to use selvages in your quilting work. The weave on them is basically more close than the rest of the surface and it used to ensure about the surface as it encounters the collecting methodology. It was not expected to be used in our endeavors.

In the photo underneath, you can see that my wrinkle reward is significantly more broad than what I would use for piecing squares. I'm basically using one of the guidelines on the line plate. The join plate has a huge amount of markings, so it's that easy to get an increasingly broad and consistent wrinkle payment.

Using the lines on the join plate as a manual for sew an increasingly broad wrinkle

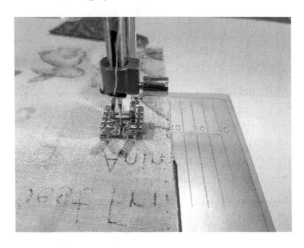

7. The power of concealing

I'm going astray from the sewing machine for a little second. I expected to set up this undertaking in light of the fact that there's something I have to bestow to you from a piecing perspective. In the first place, I expected to pick a surface and thought I'd share the method with you.

These are a couple of squares I made various years back. Some wonky stars. By and by it's a perfect chance to get them sewn together into a cover.

There's a white sashing running between all the squares, anyway I expected to have a little diminish edge around all of the squares before I sewed the sashing in. I know nothing, for example, tangling matters when you're endeavoring to clean up an endeavor.

I'm an amazingly visual individual and the best way to deal with pick surface is to put the squares on an arrangement divider and tryout the choices.

Wonky star squares

I encountered my save and picked a couple of surfaces I thought may work. I put the surfaces under a couple of the squares to help me with picking the surface I favored best for the edge. I imagine that its less complex to have all the decisions up in the first place and subsequently independently, they get shed.

A couple of decisions for the diminish packaging around the wonky star squares.

I like the end system as I consider most us do. It simply is apparently less difficult to choose the decisions we couldn't care less for and preferably we're left with the elective we like.

I couldn't have cared less for this one regardless of the way that I like the quality of the blue, it basically doesn't seem to work. Unreasonably mottled?

Blue surface that is nonsensically mottled for the packaging?

Dull is preposterously obvious for the awe inspiring squares.

It's not awful, anyway that spot has a past vibe and now and again misses the mark for the quality of the surfaces in the squares.

Blue spot surface has a substitute style to it than the absorbed tones the wonky star square.

While I like this one, it blends in a great deal with a segment of the surfaces in the squares.

A significant maritime power with a touch of a lighter, increasingly splendid blue. The principle issue? I need something else. Regardless, it made me search somewhere else and I found the perfect surface.

A perfect fit for the square edge – a dull blue with just a scramble of lighter blue.

Organize the pieces of the deals

A comparative way that it's fundamental to evaluate those edges, it's critical that the binding you add to squares be a comparative length. These squares have all been squared to 9½". Regardless, if I were to just sew portions of surface to the squares and evacuate the excess, my squares would not be the correct size when I'm set. They likely wouldn't be a comparable size either. I'm cutting the edges to the particular estimation and pin them (with my fingers). Guaranteed, the squares will all be a comparative size when I'm set.

"Pin" the pieces of the deals with your fingers.

You should be mindful when sewing these particularly confined strips (cut 1″). Any deviation on the wrinkle settlement will make that restricted strip look unusual.

I managed two squares in a steady progression and chain pieced them. This constrained a chance to sew them and the amount of strings to cut off. These are just adequate sewing practices.

Twisted or bended creases

The twofold wedding ring quilt with its twisted wrinkles is a test to sew as you can't chain piece this adjustment.

Each and every wrinkle must be stopped and started, you can't sew through the completion of the wrinkle payment. It's definitely not hard to use the FIX take a shot at the Opal 690Q to catch the beginning and end of the wrinkles. These squares have been sewn on different machines with the last item being fundamentally extraordinary. Why? That Quilter's ¼" Presser Foot made the sewing straightforward as I used the foot as my guide, not a setting on the sewing machine. I didn't require an exorbitant, nonexclusive twisted piecing foot.

For twisted wrinkles, I facilitate the center centers, place one pin to hold the two networks together. By then circumspectly head around the beginning. See how I use the quilter's drill to control the two edges of the wrinkle. This kind of wrinkle is so common – it's essentially fiddly considering the way that you have to stop and head close to the beginning and end of each wrinkle.

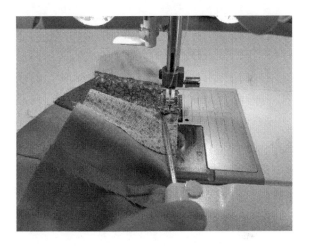

Using the quilter's bit to keep the two twisted edges together.

It's a test to sew this wrinkle as I need to get into that tight area and start where the past line of sewing wrapped up.

Wrinkles on fleece quilts

One other wrinkle I'm working on is one for a fleece quilt. I'm regardless of everything using a ¼" wrinkle reward. The fleece I'm using is worthy quality and considering the way that it was cut with a sharp turning shaper front line, there's irrelevant fraying.

In any case, I should change the line length to 2.5 rather than 2.0. The surfaces are thicker and the shorter secure length isn't as helpful for the fleece. I'll use the Exclusive Sewing Advisor to set the surface load to Medium. That normally changes the join length to 2.5 and adjusts the weight.

Because of the thicker surfaces, the Sensor Foot and the Needle Up/Down limit are so helpful. The two surfaces can be pushed straight up to the needle so there's less chance that the best one will descend.

The thicker surfaces moreover mean I'll likely need to change where I hold the edges of my surface near with the edge of the Quilter's ¼" Piecing Foot. The thicker surface suggests there will be more surface "lost" when the wrinkle payment is crushed to the opposite side. A fairly tinier wrinkle settlement will be required. I'll basically arrange the edges of the wrinkles a smidgen aside of the edge of the foot.

The Sensor Foot makes it easy to push the accompanying pieces to sew straightforwardly against the needle

The Exclusive Sewing Advisor makes all the crucial changes when the weight of the surface is changed.

CHAPTER FOUR

DRAFTING A QUILT BLOCK DESIGN

The underlying advance to organizing your own quilt structure

Steps to Drafting a Quilt Block Design

You will require several essential supplies to start:

- Graph paper

- Pencil and eraser

- Ruler

- Inspiration

- Possibly a calculator

In this model, our inspiration is a photograph of a cover.

If you have Electric Quilt programming (it shows up in a Mac interpretation, too) you can substitute it for the outline paper, pencil and eraser.

I'm correct currently using EQ7, yet some of the time I come back to antiquated paper and pencil...sometimes that is absolute less complex!

Stage 1: Identify the cross section

To draft the square you need to recognize what 'cross section' it is drawn on. Disregarding the way that it isn't evaluated in inches or centimeters, perceiving the system is a crucial bit of making sense of what sizes to cut your patches.

At the point when the square is drafted on a system, it's easy to change square sizes as you will see. In case you pick one that is spinning shaper genial, you won't need to redraft the square, anyway simply do a substitute course of action of clear math tallies.

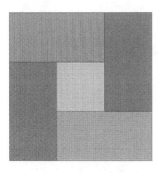

This particular arrangement is a minor takeoff from the clear square called 'Turned' (showed right) where pieced rectangular units are exchanged for the solid ones (exhibited as follows).

In the certifiable picture of the sweeping, no doubt there are three of these squares across in each line.

When drafted, the square from the sweeping looks like this...

I've used different shades of diminish to address the 'crudeness' of the square without diverting your thought by using tones or surfaces.

By and by look for the humblest fix. (This is commonly the least requesting way to deal with ascertain the grid.) In this event the tiniest fix is the center square.

Directly count what number of center squares it would take to go across and everywhere throughout the design...for our model it's 9 units which makes it a 9x9 structure.

Stage 2: Identify the units inside the sweeping square structure

A large portion of interlaced structures are contained repeated, essential units.

Separate the structure into these components.This one contains two related, anyway remarkable, sub-squares.

The center one is involved an inside fix, 2 side and 2 top/base fixes and makes a square that is 3x3 GUs...

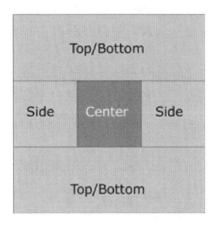

The pieced center is enclosed by four rectangular units that are moreover made of a center with two side and two top/base patches, anyway a bit of the fix sizes differentiate. This square shape is 6x3 cross section units.

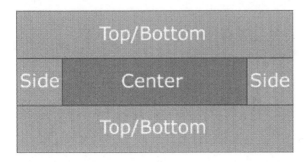

Stage 3: Choose the finished square gauge and process the fix estimations

Pick a finished square estimations. By then confine this

number by the amount of system units (GU).

For our model square, assume we need a 9" finished square. So isolated 9" (wrapped up) by 9 (the amount of GU) and we get a 1" GU.

Exactly when this number is a turning shaper pleasing number, all that is left to do is find out the fix estimations. There's no convincing motivation to draft a lifesized square.

Use this direct forumula to choose fix sizes for squares and square shapes:

Single Fold Binding

This kind of legitimate, as the name propose, covers the sweeping's edges with a single layer of surface. It might be made of either tendency or straight grain strips. It's definitely not hard to join. Helpful for quilts that will be used carefully and washed infrequently. Helpful for divider quilts.

Self-official (to a great extent called Edge-turned Binding)

This kind of limiting protects the sweeping's edges with just a singular layer of surface. For this system, the sweeping's supporting surface is sliced straight and collapsed over to the front of the cover and closed set up to shape the definitive. Helpful for quilts that will be used gently and washed seldom. Valuable for divider quilts.

Monetarily made Binding Tape

Precut and packaged inclination confining tape: Black twofold wrinkle (l), White single overlay (r)

Fiscally made legitimate can be an exceptional productive gadget, if you pick the right one. There are two sorts:

• Precut and Packaged Binding Tape: This is sold as an idea in surface stores. Do whatever it takes not to use this for quilts. This coupling is made of surface half polyester/half cotton and is uncommon in quality than your ordinary cover surface. It keeps an eye out for not lay level after it's been washed. Save this for finishing youngster jaw wipers, covers, wrinkles in dress, etc.

• Precut Bias Quilt Binding on Rolls: This kind of limiting is made and given by a comparable maker's that produce the quality cover surface you'll find in your local quilt store. The two drawbacks are:

1. A compelled choice of tones and models

2. A compelled choice of limiting widths

THE END

Manufactured by Amazon.ca
Bolton, ON